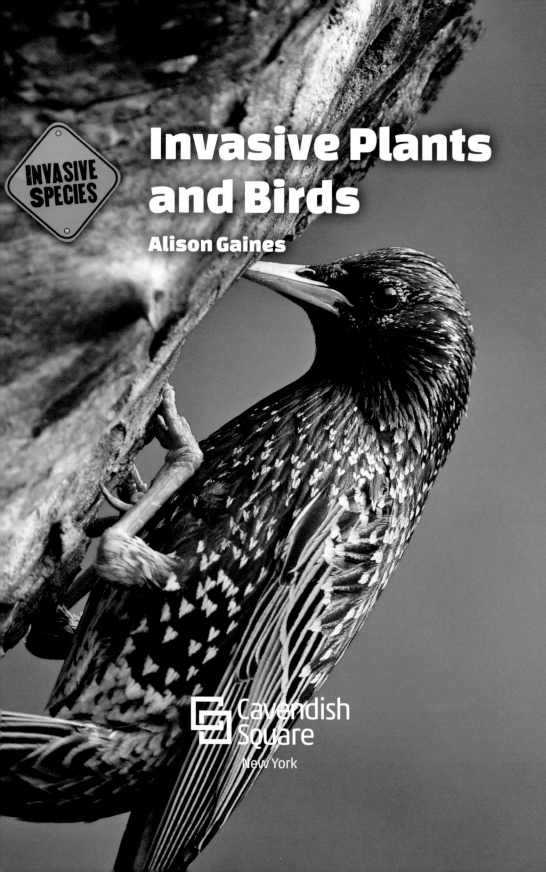

INVASIVE SPECIES

Invasive Plants and Birds

Alison Gaines

Cavendish Square

New York

Published in 2017 by Cavendish Square Publishing, LLC
243 5th Avenue, Suite 136, New York, NY 10016

Library of Congress Cataloging-in-Publication Data

Names: Gaines, Alison, author.
Title: Invasive plants and birds / Alison Gaines.
Other titles: Invasive species (Cavendish Square Publishing)
Description: New York : Cavendish Square Publishing, [2017] | Series: Invasive species | Includes bibliographical references and index.
Identifiers: LCCN 2016004063 (print) | LCCN 2016008804 (ebook) | ISBN 9781502618344 (library bound) | ISBN 9781502618368 (ebook)
Subjects: LCSH: Introduced birds--Juvenile literature. | Invasive plants--Juvenile literature. | Introduced organisms--Juvenile literature. | Biotic communities--Juvenile literature.
Classification: LCC QL677.79.I58 G35 2017 (print) | LCC QL677.79.I58 (ebook) | DDC 578.6/2--dc23
LC record available at http://lccn.loc.gov/2016004063

Editorial Director: David McNamara
Editor: Renni Johnson
Copy Editor: Nathan Heidelberger
Art Director: Jeffrey Talbot
Designer: Alan Sliwinski
Production Assistant: Karol Szymczuk
Photo Research: J8 Media

Printed in the United States of America

CONTENTS

Invasive Plants and Birds

Water hyacinths are popular decorative plants in garden ponds. One plant can produce up to five thousand seeds.

Flying, Creeping, Growing

★ ★ ★ ★ ★

Where is home for you? Are you native to a certain place, such as your hometown or home country? Do you live there now, or have you moved somewhere new? Humans are very adaptable and can survive in many different places and on different diets. Birds and plants have native habitats, specific places where they thrive and where they have the food and climate they need to survive. Like people, animals and plants sometimes end up far away from their homes, surrounded by different species.

Sometimes by mistake and sometimes on purpose, humans move species from one place to another.

About 10 percent of these species survive in their new environments, and they are known as **introduced** species. Of the introduced species, only 10 percent of those thrive, spreading beyond the place where they ended up and expanding into new territory. At this point, a species becomes known as **invasive**.

This book focuses on invasive birds and plants. To start, let's look at one bird you've probably seen before: the starling.

European Starling

The starling's original home is in the continents of Europe and Asia. In 1890, a man named Eugene Schieffelin brought starlings to the United States. Why? He thought it would be a good idea to bring to America each type of bird that William Shakespeare mentions in his plays. He released sixty starlings, as well as many other species, into Central Park in New York City. Most of the species he released could not survive in New York City, but the starlings did.

The starlings spread like crazy across North America. Schieffelin did not know that introducing these birds could possibly have any bad effects, but the starlings quickly caused major, lasting changes for people and for other birds.

Starlings nest in cavities, or holes, in buildings or trees. As starlings multiply and take up space, other hole-nesting birds, such as bluebirds and red-headed woodpeckers, have not been able to find places to nest. Sometimes starlings even take over the nests of other birds. Starlings eat insects, berries, and seeds, and have caused problems for farmers, eating crops as well as animal feed. Like rats and pigeons, they sometimes spread diseases.

Fit to Survive

Every species has a set of needs from a habitat in order to survive, and the requirements of some plants and animals are more flexible than others. If a species is well adjusted to its home, it has a high level of **fitness**. A species that is very fit in one environment could be unfit in another.

Successful invaders have **adaptations**—tend to be more flexible, able to become fit to different environments and predators. Starlings and other invasive birds have a few things in common. They

AN INVASION UNFOLDS

Eurasia

New York, NY

A large group of starlings, like the one pictured, is called a murmuration.

Native habitat: Eurasia (Asia and Europe)

In 1890, Eugene Schieffelin brought sixty starlings to New York City and introduced them in Central Park. The next year, he released another forty.

Over the next few years, the starlings multiplied easily and spread in all directions across the country.

By 1940—just fifty years later—they could be found in every state.

Today, there are more than two hundred million starlings in North America.

are not picky eaters, so they have less trouble finding food. Birds that can cope with different climates or that aren't particular about nesting sites might do well in unfamiliar environments. Birds that reproduce quickly, laying eggs often and laying a large number of eggs at a time, also have an advantage.

Invasive plants are usually fast growers and can survive under various conditions, such as in the sun

English ivy can take over the habitats of other plants, much like it has taken over this building.

or shade, and in wet or dry places. They often have a deep root system so that damage to the aboveground part of the plant does not mean the end of its life. Also, plants that have seeds with a long **dormancy period** are successful invaders. This means that the seeds can survive underground without sprouting for a long time. Seeds with a long dormancy period might even survive a flood or fire. This also makes it more difficult to bring down invasive plant populations.

Today, invasive species often have something else in common: they tend to get along well with humans. Not all species can live with humans as their neighbors. Think of the animals you may see in your backyard or in the park: These are most likely animals that are used to the impact of human activity. How many of these familiar birds and plants are invasive?

English sparrows, or house sparrows, tend to thrive wherever humans are, often nesting in eaves or crannies of buildings.

Make Yourself at Home

★ ★ ★ ★ ★

magine, again, where you live. For plants and animals, this is called their habitat. Has your habitat ever been disrupted? How did you adapt, or adjust? Maybe you had company visiting, so you had to sleep in a different room. Did you sleep as well in a different room? Maybe the power went out so you had to use candles. Was it more difficult to get things done? All over the world, plants and animals have their habitats disrupted. In some cases, invasive species are the cause. If a native species struggles to adapt to the changes in its habitat, its future could be in danger.

Alien species might have an easier time invading some places than others. Islands, especially, have very fragile environments and have been troubled by invasions throughout history. Because islands are small and isolated, there may not be room for the native and non-native species to coexist. Species living on islands are well-adapted to their particular home but may not be prepared to deal with outsiders.

When an invader enters an **ecosystem**, it will compete with native species for space, food, and water. An invasive plant does more than just crowd out other plants. It can change the whole ecosystem. It might change the hydrology, or wetness or dryness, of the soil, reducing the water supply left for the native plants. It could also change the fire regime, making the whole region more or less susceptible to a fire. Invasive plants might compete with native ones for sunlight.

Troublesome Plants

Cheatgrass was introduced to North America from Eurasia in the late 1800s. It spread in the American Southwest where native shrubs, like sagebrush, also live. Besides competing with native plants for space,

INVADING HAWAII

The Hawaiian Islands have long struggled with invasive birds, which first came to the islands as pets of Western colonists. Two such birds are the red-vented bulbul and the red-whiskered bulbul, both native to Asia. They were brought to the islands as pets, and either escaped or were illegally released in the 1950s and 1960s. They are aggressive toward native birds and compete with them for food and habitat. They eat fruit and vegetable crops, and through their droppings, they can help spread plant seeds, native and invasive, across the island. Many other birds were introduced in this same way in Hawaii and cause similar problems.

The red-vented bulbul gets its name from the bright red patch under its tail.

and invading crops like wheat, cheatgrass is highly flammable, making fires more likely. The sagebrush, which has not evolved to be fire-resistant, does not thrive with this new neighbor.

Sometimes an invasive species disrupts a native habitat in more bizarre ways. Bitterbush is a shrub native to Central and South America that has spread to many places, including the Greater St. Lucia Wetland

Able to grow in these dry conditions, bitterbush is a problem because of the shadow it casts.

NATIVE OR INVASIVE?

In the Pacific Northwest, the spotted owl has been a symbol of **conservation**, the effort to keep native species alive and safe. Native to the region, spotted owls require old-growth forests, often large redwoods and Douglas firs, to build their nests. Old-growth forests are areas of rich **biodiversity**, old trees, and relatively little human disturbance. Today, these forests are dwindling because of logging and housing developments. The spotted owl faces the threat of habitat loss because of humans, and on top of that, it has to compete with other species coming into the area. One such species is the barred owl.

The barred owl is common and widespread (and native) in the eastern half of the United States and Canada. In the past few decades, some have been making their way from Canada into the territory of spotted owls, competing for food and, most importantly, nesting space. Like many invaders, it is more aggressive and more adaptable than its fragile cousin. It can nest in a variety of habitats and does not specifically need the old-growth trees. Because the invasion of the barred owl could be considered a natural migration, though aided by human activity, some biologists call the barred owl a "native-invasive."

Park in South Africa. It grows densely and quickly, taking up space and sunlight that other plants need.

Plants aren't the only victims of bitterbush's invasion. Nile crocodiles nest in the St. Lucia Wetland Park and need open, sandy areas with full sunlight to lay their eggs. Bitterbush can obstruct areas that would otherwise be ideal for nesting. Sometimes it grows over an existing nest, casting shade and keeping

Even crocodiles are susceptible to invasive species affecting their habitat and nesting grounds.

the nest cooler than it would be in the full sun. Did you know that the sex of baby crocodiles depends on the temperature of the eggs? Eggs kept at a cooler temperature usually produce females, so the eggs that have been shaded by the bitterbush will hatch mostly girls. In order for a population to stay strong and keep reproducing, there needs to be a balance of both males and females, so the lowly bitterbush is causing a real problem for the population of the crocodile, which is a mighty predator along the Nile.

INVADERS THROUGHOUT THE WORLD

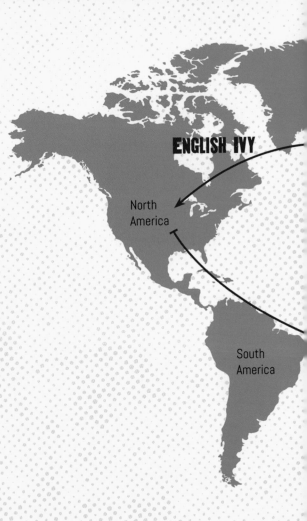

North America
Kudzu vine
European starling
House sparrow
English ivy
Red-vented bulbul
Red-whiskered bulbul
Rubber vine
Saltcedar
Cheatgrass
Yellow starthistle

South America
Smooth-billed ani
   (in Galápagos)
House sparrow
Mysore raspberry

Europe
Water hyacinth

Africa
Bitterbush
House sparrow
Prickly pear cactus

ENGLISH IVY

North America

South America

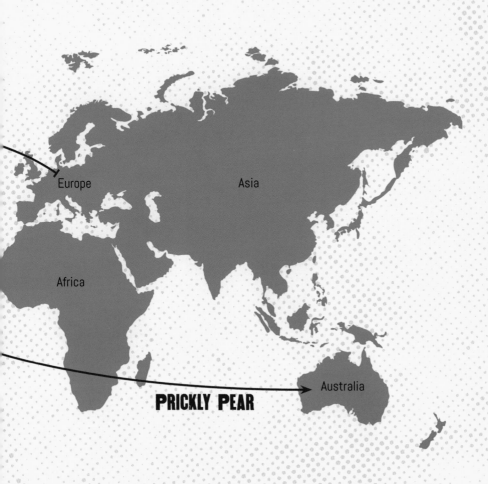

Europe

Asia

Africa

PRICKLY PEAR ➝ Australia

Asia
Rubber vine

Australia
Prickly pear cactus
House sparrow
Rubber vine

Backyard bird feeders attract native birds like these house finches (native to North America) as well as invasive ones.

Humans: Helping or Hurting?

★ ★ ★ ★ ★

Humans introduce species for many reasons. It's hard to foresee all the changes that a new plant or animal will bring. When humans fail to control the new population, the invasive species cause unpredictable damage.

Throughout history, most introductions have been for food, for humans and for livestock. In fact, many of the popular crops in the United States are not native. For instance, wheat is believed to have originated in southwestern Asia and was grown in America for the first time in 1602. Wheat and other introduced crops are not considered invasive, though, because they do not expand their range without human help.

Sometimes plants are introduced to stop **erosion**. Erosion is when land is worn away over time by water, wind, or from people and animals walking on it. Having a plant's root system in the earth can keep the earth from wearing down, so sometimes people introduce a plant, a **soil stabilizer**, that will help with this.

The Vine That Ate the South

The kudzu vine is a massive example of good intentions gone bad. It is native to Asia and was brought to the United States in 1876 as part of the Japanese exhibit at the Philadelphia Centennial Exhibition. Visitors to the exhibit admired the vine's creeping abilities and its attractive purple flowers. They thought to use it to decorate their houses and create shade for their porches. Later on, people decided to use it as food for cattle and to control erosion. While it prefers full sunlight, kudzu is very hardy and can survive in various weather and sunlight conditions. Its roots can extend as deep as 12 feet (3.7 meters) into the soil, meaning that the plant gets nutrients easily and is hard to kill. In the spring and summer, it can grow up to 1 foot (0.3 m) per day!

FASHIONABLE INVASIONS

People used to introduce species on purpose because it was fashionable. In the 1700s and 1800s, acclimatization societies were formed by people with the intention of bringing new species into their home nations to create an ideal environment. Eugene Schieffelin, who brought the starling to New York, was a member of the American Acclimatization Society. Some of the world's most harmful plant invaders, such as the rubber vine native to Madagascar, were introduced for decoration.

At the same time, the British colonized other parts of the world, including India. Colonists transplanted species to make their new homes resemble the old, building English gardens, with species like hollyhock, cowslip, and violets.

People used to think that nature existed for their exploitation and enjoyment. Today, people are more careful, having seen the damage caused by introduced species.

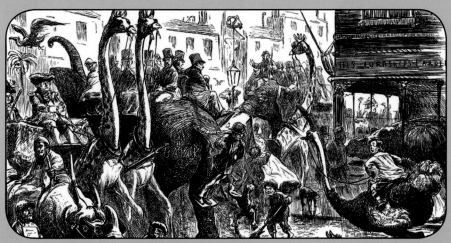

This drawing represents what acclimatization societies imagined their towns could be like, with species gathered from afar.

Planting kudzu is now illegal in the United States because it is a major pest, especially for farmers and loggers. It will grow over almost anything in its path. Areas that have been taken over by kudzu look like they are covered in a green, fuzzy blanket. In its native range in Asia, kudzu survives but does not take over the way it does in the American South. In Asia, kudzu has to compete with the other species in its native habitat, which keep it in check. But in

Because kudzu has so few natural competitors in North America, it will take over pretty much anything in its path.

America, kudzu has few competitors and is able to dominate its new ecosystem. The vine actually seems to prefer disturbed areas where humans have already been at work manipulating the environment through logging, farming, and construction. When they alter an environment, humans can help invasive species without realizing, making it that much easier for an invader like kuzdu to take over.

Putting Down Roots

Of course, sometimes humans introduce species unintentionally. Plants are especially easy to introduce because their seeds are **hitchhikers**. Without realizing, people can carry seeds to new places on clothes or in suitcases, down the street or to new continents by planes and boats.

Plants often reach new locations through hay. Ranchers will purchase hay because their animals may need more nutrients than their grazing area provides. The hay is made from alfalfa, but parts of other weeds can make their way into these bales. When the bales arrive at their new location, seeds end up in the ground and can germinate. Animals and birds eat plants and pass seeds through their system, dropping invasive species in new locations.

The yellow starthistle, native to Eurasia, was introduced to the United States through hay bales. It has very deep roots and produces many seeds, making it difficult to get rid of. While people have tried to control invasive plants by allowing livestock to graze on them, this is not an option with yellow starthistle. Its pointy spines make it painful to eat. Worse, if the starthistle is present in a habitat, animals have to eat more of other plants, perhaps native ones, that don't have the painful spines. People have found several ways to keep the population down, such as introducing specific insects that feed on the thistle.

Today, people are much more aware of the dangers of introducing species, and of how to avoid it. But there is more international travel and trade happening today than ever before. If you ever travel internationally, you have to fill out a customs form declaring any animal or plant matter you are carrying with you. Governments take these measures to make sure that you don't bring any unwanted invaders into your destination.

FEED THE BIRDS?

A red-breasted nuthatch, used to feeding upside down, enjoys a suet feeder.

People who enjoy bird watching often install bird feeders in their yards. Feeders might attract birds who are tired from migrating, allowing them to rest and eat. However, any bird feeder owner knows that they run the risk of attracting and feeding invasive birds as well as native ones. Often, house sparrows and starlings take over a feeder, and the less aggressive natives don't get a chance to eat.

Some companies make bird feeders designed to keep squirrels (another invasive species to North America) and larger birds out. Some suet feeders are designed so that only birds that feed upside down can get at the food. While starlings can do many things, they cannot eat upside down!

It is exciting to see native birds at the feeder. Just a few native birds that are relatively common across the United States include goldfinches, chickadees, nuthatches, the American robin, the northern flicker, the northern cardinal in the East, and the spotted towhee in the west. If you have a bird feeder, consider finding a bird book and making a list of how many birds come to visit.

Saltcedar

Scientific Name: *Tamarix ramosissima, Tamarix chinensis, Tamarix parviflora*

Description: Three different species, each of which is a woody shrub. Looks like a cedar tree with white to pink flowers. Can grow up to 30 feet (9 m).

Origin: The Mediterranean region and Asia.

New Habitat: Invasive in the American Southwest, especially Arizona and New Mexico.

Relocation: Introduced by the US government in the 1800s to control erosion.

Adaptations: Different strains of saltcedar have developed in the past two centuries. Some of these have hybridized with each other, making a new strain—a hybrid—that is more acclimated to the dry Southwestern environment.

Effects on New Habitat: The leaves contain salt, making the soil saltier when they fall to the ground. Soil then becomes poisonous for other plants. In this way, native trees, such as cottonwood, willow, and mesquite, have suffered. Out-competes other plants for water. Crowds out native trees and the birds that rely on them.

House Sparrow

Scientific Name: *Passer domesticus*

Description: Small, brown bird with a beige-colored breast and chestnut-colored back. Females are lighter and males have a black bib on their chests. Social and not shy around humans.

Diet: Variety of grains, seeds, invertebrates, vegetation, bread (and other food humans throw away).

Origin: Believed to have originated in Africa about 8.5 million years ago. Different subspecies established themselves in different parts of the world. The most successful one made Europe and Asia its home.

New Habitat: All continents except Antarctica. Considered the most common bird in the world besides the chicken. Especially prevalent in urban areas.

Relocation: Introduced in the United States for pest control and because sparrows were popular at the time. Traveled to other continents on its own.

Adaptations: Have adapted to rely on humans being nearby for food and places to nest. Do not migrate in the winter, which is unusual for sparrows, surviving with help from human activity.

Effects on New Habitat: Aggressive toward native birds, outcompeting them for food and nesting sites.

Prickly Pear Cactus

Scientific Name: *Opuntia stricta*

Description: A cactus that can grow up to 6 feet (1.8 m) tall, made of flat, circular, spiny pods. Produces reddish-purple fruits and yellow flowers.

Origin: Northern South America to the southern United States.

New Habitat: Present in all continents except Antarctica. Invasive in Australia, parts of the Caribbean,

South Africa, Spain, Madagascar, Morocco, Namibia, Tunisia, Yemen, and India.

Relocation: In the case of Australia, brought by British colonists in 1788. Used as a natural cattle fence, as well as a decorative plant. Seeds continue to spread by grazing animals, birds, and through the trade of cacti as ornamental plants.

Adaptations: Only grows on sandy soil in its native habitat, but invading populations have adapted to different types of soil.

Effects on new habitat: Makes land unsuitable for farming. By 1900, it was estimated that the cactus had taken over 10 million acres (4 million hectares) of land near its introduction site in Australia. Competes with other cacti in the *Opuntia* genus. Use of the cactoblastis moth to bring down populations has had unintended effects on native populations as well as invasive ones.

Smooth-Billed Ani

Scientific Name: *Crotophaga ani*

Description: A little larger than a starling. Black feathers and a large bill.

Diet: Insects, small lizards, fruits.

Origin: Caribbean and mainland South America.

New habitat: Galápagos Islands, about 600 miles (966 kilometers) off the coast of Ecuador.

Relocation: Likely introduced by ranchers in 1960s to control cattle ticks.

Adaptations: Managed to spread between islands. Likes to live in groups.

Effects on new habitat: Islands are especially vulnerable. Competes with native birds (like the Galápagos finches, which helped Charles Darwin learn about adaptation). Spreads seeds of some invasive plants, like mysore raspberry.

STAY ON PATH

By straying from the path, visitors could step on living plants, or introduce other species without knowing it.

Lending Nature a Hand

★ ★ **★** ★ ★

Humans are usually at least partly responsible for harmful invasions, so it is also our responsibility to attempt to control any negative effects that these invasions have. How best to do this is not always clear.

Usually, invasive species thrive because humans have upset the natural order in some way. However, it is hard for humans to step in and try to control the damage without upsetting nature even further. When a species is recognized as invasive and harmful, often the first idea is to attack the invasive species itself. Journalist Garry Hamilton uses the example of weeds. If weeds are taking over a native habitat, it might seem logical to poison them. However, what other problems could this solution be causing? Also, this solution ignores the question of how the weeds ended up there in the first place.

If humans put more energy toward preventing the spread of harmful species, there would be fewer invasions to worry about in the future. Taking care of the environment in this way is called **environmental stewardship**.

In the meantime, invasive species are destroying habitats as we speak, and biologists are at work trying to control the invasions in progress. Land managers have several different tools for dealing with invasive plants. They include **mechanical control**, **chemical control**, **biological control**, **controlled burns**, and **reseeding**.

- Mechanical control: Using farming tools to remove harmful plants by hand.
- Chemical control: Using herbicides (poisons) that will kill the invasive plant. This runs the risk of harming other native plants as well.
- Biological control: Releasing a predator of the invasive species to eat or outcompete the plant.

- Controlled burns: Purposefully starting fires that reinvigorate native plants, which are adapted to survive fires, and remove young invasive plants.
- Reseeding, or revegetating: Planting native species after an invasive species has been removed.

Plants and birds go hand in hand much of the time. An invasion by plants can be dangerous not just to other plants but to other species such as birds that eat or make homes from plant life. While invasive birds have been known to adapt, native birds tend to rely on native plants for their nesting and feeding, just like the spotted owl relies on the native old growth conifers in the Pacific Northwest.

Humans do not have a very good track record when it comes to predicting which species might become invasive. Also, some argue that we look at invasive species in the wrong way. As more species move around the globe, with and without human help, the world is becoming less diverse and locally unique. The world is one massive biodiverse environment, meaning that it can support many different life-forms across the globe. Invasive species are dangerous because they threaten biodiversity, crowding out more fragile species and making the different ecosystems of the world more similar.

Some scientists argue that the Earth is always changing, and that invasive species are part of normal environmental change, with species like kudzu vine and house sparrows taking over across the globe. If the spread of certain dominant species is inevitable, some fragile native species won't survive.

STARTING FIRES TO RESTART LIFE

Many ecosystems depend on the occasional fire to keep their populations healthy. This may seem backward because for humans, fires are usually disasters. However, land managers conduct controlled burns in areas that need help maintaining their biodiversity.

Fires can help trees become healthier by removing lower branches, helping the tree grow new branches. Fires remove a lot of leaves and needles that create shade, allowing sunlight to reach young plants. The ash puts more nutrients into the soil. After the controlled burn, land managers will remove seedlings of invasive plants, which are now easier to get to. They might also reseed with native plants. For a time, these areas need to be monitored for invasive plants returning through dormant seeds that weren't destroyed.

GLOSSARY

adaptation The ability of species to change as their environment changes. Species evolve physically through generations or they develop new habits.

biodiversity The idea that a healthy ecosystem is one with a variety of animals, none outcompeting each other.

biological control The practice of controlling an invasive species by introducing a predator of the species.

chemical control The practice of using poisons, such as herbicides, to kill invasive plants.

conservation The practice of preserving ecosystems to support native species and to limit human impact.

controlled burn The practice of lighting a fire in a specific area to regenerate native species and control invasives.

dormancy period The length of time that a seed can remain alive without sprouting.

ecosystem A community made up of different organisms that all contribute to it.

environmental stewardship The practice of taking care of the Earth and its fragile ecosystems.

erosion The effect of land being washed or blown away by wind or water over time, or worn down by human activity.

fitness The ability of a species to survive in a given environment.

hitchhikers Seeds or other tiny organisms that spread by "hitching a ride" to a new location on people's clothes, animals' fur, the ballast water of boats, and more.

introduced A species brought to a new ecosystem with human help. Not all introduced species are invasive.

invasive An introduced species that grows steeply in population, spreads to new areas, and causes problems for native species.

mechanical control The practice of removing invasive plants by hand, using farming tools or hand-pulling.

reseeding Also called revegetating. The practice of adding seeds or seedlings of a native plant to an area, in hopes that an invader will have a harder time invading.

soil stabilizer A plant that was planted to control erosion.

FIND OUT MORE

Books

Chaline, Eric. *Fifty Animals That Changed the Course of History*. Buffalo: Firefly Books, 2011.

Hamilton, Garry. *Super Species: The Creatures That Will Dominate the Planet*. Buffalo: Firefly Books, 2010.

May, Suellen. *Invasive Terrestrial Plants*. New York: Infobase Publishing, 2007.

Websites

All About Birds

www.allaboutbirds.org.
This website is a great resource for birders of any age. Identify and learn more about the birds in your backyard, including whether they are native to your area. There is information on house sparrows and starlings as well as other pests and predators that threaten native birds and what humans can do to help.

Invasives: What About Weeds?

weedinvasion.org/pdfs/extras/extras/what_about_weeds.pdf
This website offers resources for teachers on invasive plants.
This worksheet provides a good explanation on the definition
of weeds, how they spread, and problems they cause.

View 100 of the World's Worst Invasive Alien Species

issg.org/worst100_species.html
This website has a list of one hundred of the world's most
harmful invasive species—including birds, plants, and many
others. Click on the photo of the species you're interested
in to read its profile. The impact info details the species'
history as an invader.

INDEX

Page numbers in **boldface** are illustrations. Entries in **boldface** are glossary terms.

ABOUT THE AUTHOR

Alison Gaines has a bachelor of arts in creative writing from Knox College and enjoys writing educational books for young readers, as well as poems. She is especially grateful to her parents, who are both ornithologists, for raising her with an appreciation for nature and native species. She lives in Chicago, and when she is not writing, she enjoys playing the cello and attending classical music concerts.